LAST BREATHS OF STEAM

COMMEMORATING THE THIRTIETH ANNIVERSARY OF THE END OF BR STEAM

Michael S Welch

RUNPAST PUBLISHING

© Michael S Welch 1998

Published by Runpast Publishing, 10 Kingscote Grove, Cheltenham, Gloucestershire GL51 6JX

Typesetting and reproduction by Viners Wood Associates – 01452 812813
Printed in England by The Amadeus Press Ltd., Huddersfield

ISBN 1 870754 44 1

Title page photograph: Against all expectations, 'A4' Class Pacifics continued to work the Glasgow to Aberdeen trains into 1966, but the withdrawal of No.60007 *Sir Nigel Gresley* in February meant that only five engines – Nos.60004, 60009, 60019, 60024 and 60034 – were available. Time was increasingly spent under repair with parts being cannibalised from withdrawn engines. In addition, railtour duties – one trip involved No.60024 *Kingfisher* visiting Weymouth – sometimes took locomotives away for a week or more. In April 1966, a diesel diagram on the 8.25am Glasgow to Aberdeen and 5.15pm return reverted to 'A4' power and these trains were particularly well patronised by enthusiasts. But only three 'A4's lasted into the summer and in July a crisis occurred when all the survivors were 'stopped' simultaneously. The ScR operating authorities immediately called upon the services of No.60532 *Blue Peter*, one of the three remaining 'A2's, which was hastily moved from Dundee to Ferryhill and pressed into use, generally on the 1.30pm ex-Aberdeen and 11.2pm return from Glasgow. *Blue Peter* had seen only sporadic use at Dundee where, together with sister engine Nos.60528 *Tudor Minstrel* and 60530 *Sayajirao*, it was usually on stand-by duty or working freight trains, so the rare opportunity of seeing an 'A2' regularly in action was welcome compensation for the scarcity of 'A4's! *Blue Peter* was pictured at Perth on 25th July 1966, while powering 'The Grampian' (1.30pm ex-Aberdeen), which was one of the slower trains on the route, taking four hours for the journey from Aberdeen to Glasgow. *K. M. Falconer*

Front cover photograph: On 31st December 1967 Carlisle Kingmoor depot closed, and the familiar sight of steam traction, which had been part of the Border City's heritage for over 130 years, came to an end. To mark this sad event BR Standard 'Britannia' Pacific No.70013 *Oliver Cromwell*, which was specially groomed for the occasion, was turned out to work the 9.45am Boxing Day football special to Blackpool South, and is seen here at Lytham, just outside Blackpool. On the return journey, Grayrigg bank was topped at about 20mph and a stop for water was made at Tebay. The enginemen expected a banker to be provided for the ascent of Shap, but none was available so *Oliver Cromwell* took its 451-ton, thirteen-coach load up the bank unassisted, speed being about 10mph at the summit. This train proved to be the last steam passenger working over Shap, apart from railtours using preserved locomotives. *Peter Fitton*

Back cover photograph: On 4th August 1968, the official last day of steam, a number of society specials criss-crossed the north west of England, which left the way clear for BR's own commemorative run a week later. This will probably be best remembered for the exorbitant fare demanded, rather than the route or motive power, and the infamous 'Fifteen Guinea Special' of 11th August 1968 has since become part of railway folklore. For the record the train started from Liverpool, coincidentally not far from the site of the Rainhill trials, and proceeded to Carlisle via Manchester, Blackburn and the Settle & Carlisle line. Two Stanier 'Black Fives', Nos.44871 and 44781, were provided for the return run by the same route, and the pair are seen near Helm, south of Appleby. It may have been a totally artificial event, but at least the special was headed by a locomotive combination which must have been witnessed many times over the S&C, and, unbelievably, the sun shone for this historic trip. Long live steam! *J. Spencer Gilks*

INTRODUCTION

In the February 1967 edition of the 'Railway Observer', the authoritative journal of the Railway Correspondence & Travel Society, it was reported that 129 active steam locomotives were based at Carlisle Kingmoor shed, the last remaining steam depot in the city. The depot's allocation included more than 30 BR Standard 'Britannia' Pacifics and two dozen Class '9F' 2-10-0s. During the summer of that year, steam traction was well in evidence along the northern part of the West Coast main line on both freight and passenger workings and Kingmoor shed, over which a continuous pall of smoke seemed to hang, was doubtless a hive of activity. But dieselisation was proceeding so rapidly that by the end of the year Kingmoor depot was closed, and the Westmorland fells would no longer echo to the sound of steam locomotives doing battle with the four miles of 1 in 75 gradient from Tebay to Shap Summit. Steam traction was also eliminated from the wonderfully scenic Settle & Carlisle line at the same time. From the New Year steam was confined to its last refuge in north west England.

Steam's rapid retreat from Carlisle was typical of the almost indecent haste with which BR strove to rid itself of steam traction throughout the 1960s. During this period there was a headlong rush to dieselise, and this policy, combined with the effects of the Beeching Plan of extensive line closures, ensured that in little over ten years BR was transformed from an almost all steam railway, into one operated entirely by modern traction. Sadly, many steam engines which were less than ten years old were sacrificed in the rush to dieselise, but some of the diesel classes which replaced them were so unreliable that they saw even less service than the steam engines. Some transformation!

This album, which has been published to commemorate the thirtieth anniversary of the end of steam, attempts to document the decline of steam traction during its final five years or so of BR service, until the inevitable end came in August 1968. Hopefully, it will rekindle many memories for enthusiasts who painfully witnessed the sad, systematic destruction of the steam locomotive during that period. I have attempted to illustrate most of the landmarks during steam's rapid decline and, in order to achieve this, have contacted many talented photographers up and down the country, without whose unfailing cooperation production of this album would not have been possible. I am most grateful to those who have made their irreplaceable colour transparencies available for publication in this volume. The pictures have been arranged as far as possible in chronological order, but in some cases photographers were unsure of the precise date certain photographs were taken, so occasionally I had to resort to guesswork. Finally, I would like to thank Hugh Ballantyne, Terence A. Barry, David J. Fakes, Peter Fitton, Graham Mallinson and Neville Simms who kindly assisted during the production of this volume.

M.S.W.
Burgess Hill, West Sussex. *January 1998*

The LMSR 'Coronation' Class 8P Pacifics were (at least in the author's opinion!) the finest steam locomotives ever to run in Great Britain and in this picture No.46245 *City of London* is seen passing Broughton, north of Preston, with the down 'Lakes Express' on a sunny 22nd June 1963. Built in June 1943, No.6245 emerged in wartime black livery and was named by the Lord Mayor of London at a ceremony at Euston Station on 20th July 1943. Some members of the class had already been withdrawn by the time this shot was taken and the survivors eked out a precarious existence on a variety of turns, including freight and parcels duties or deputising for diesels. Twenty-two locomotives lasted into 1964, but in September of that year LMR headquarters issued a sad decree that the entire class must be withdrawn, with the exception of one example which was granted a short-term stay of execution for a railtour duty. No.46245 was one of three 'Coronations' hauled from Crewe to Cashmore's scrap yard at Great Bridge on 8th December 1964 and had been cut up by 19th December. *City of London* is thought to have been the last 'Coronation' to receive a general repair, in October 1962. What a waste of an absolutely magnificent locomotive!

Peter Fitton

The 4½ miles long branch from Havant to Hayling Island, which was opened in July 1867, will probably be best remembered for the LBSCR 'Terrier' 0-6-0Ts, which, owing to a severe weight limit on Langstone bridge, were the only engines permitted to work the line. The branch was especially busy on summer weekends, when holidaymakers flocked to the island and a very intensive service was operated. Unfortunately, in the early 1960s Langstone bridge was found to be in a deteriorating condition, and apparently required repairs costing £400,000. Closure took place from 4th November 1963 so the bridge, which had enabled the delightful 'Terriers' to survive for so long, was also the reason for the line's downfall. During the final weekend an especially augmented service was provided for passengers making a farewell trip. Five 'Terriers', which were based at Fratton, a sub-shed of Eastleigh, survived to the end, including No.32650 seen here between Havant and Langstone on 28th July 1963. The vintage 'Terrier' was subsequently bought for preservation and can be seen today on the Kent & East Sussex Railway. Note the coaches which form the train. The first vehicle is a 1930s Maunsell brake coach, which was later converted for push-pull operation, but by the date of this picture the push-pull gear was no longer in use, although the vehicle retains the end look-out windows.

David Clark

A scene at the distinctive station at Cheddar, in Somerset, on 17th August 1963 showing Ivatt Class '2MT' 2-6-2T No.41245 leaving on the 3.28pm Witham to Yatton train. This long rural branch was opened in two parts, from opposite ends. The East Somerset Railway from Witham reached Wells in 1862 whilst from the west the Yatton & Cheddar Valley Railway arrived at Cheddar in 1869 and reached Wells a year later. At the time of this picture the line had only three weeks of life remaining, closure being scheduled from 9th September. The final day of passenger services saw a selection of classes working on the line, with the 11.12am and 2.45pm Yatton to Witham and their corresponding returns being worked by Collett 0-6-0 No.3218. A BR Standard Class '3MT' 2-6-2T took an afternoon Frome to Bristol train, while the last train from Yatton to Wells was hauled by a pannier tank engine. The eastern section of this branch remains open for stone traffic, while an adjoining stretch forms the East Somerset Railway.

Hugh Ballantyne

For many years 'Britannia' Pacifics were associated with the Eastern Region, and especially the Great Eastern line from London to Norwich, where they revolutionised services. Following dieselisation of this route, the 'Britannias' drifted to other ER sheds and saw service on the East Coast route for a time, working Kings Cross to Cleethorpes trains. By 1963 most were based at either March or Immingham sheds, and were often relegated to mundane tasks. During the summer of that year, an example was often seen powering an evening Immingham to Rotherham tank train, a far cry from crack GE expresses! In this view, No.70040 *Clive of India* is seen reversing out of New Holland Pier station after arrival with the 2.27pm from Skegness, on 24th August 1963. This working was a holiday train, routed via Louth, which only ran during the height of the summer. Note the Thompson-designed non-corridor rolling stock, which looks out of place paired with a 'Britannia'. Four months later *Clive of India* was one of a batch of 'Britannias' transferred to Carlisle and it subsequently became a regular sight on the West Coast main line.

Mike Hudson

The summer of 1963 provided the last opportunity to travel behind WR steam from London to the west of England, on various Saturday holiday trains. In this picture, 'Castle' Class 4-6-0 No.7036 *Taunton Castle* is seen leaving Yatton with one of the final workings, the 9.45am Paddington to Weston-Super-Mare, on a damp Saturday 7th September. This may have been *Taunton Castle*'s swan song on passenger duty, because it was officially condemned later the same month. The 1.45pm to Wells, with Ivatt 2-6-2T No.41245 in charge, is waiting in the bay platform, on the right. This was the final day of passenger services along this attractive route. The rapid run-down of steam traction in the west was so advanced, that during the summer of 1963 Plymouth Laira shed, formerly one of the WR's principal steam depots, was reduced to just one regular steam passenger turn – a daily excursion to Goodrington, usually powered by a 'Castle'.

Hugh Ballantyne

An auto train bound for Exeter, propelled by an 0-4-2T tank, is seen leaving the picturesque station at Bampton on the Exe Valley line on 14th September 1963. This lovely line ran, as its name suggests, up the River Exe valley, from Stoke Canon (north of Exeter) to Morebath Junction, on the Taunton to Barnstaple route, a distance of 19¼ miles. The route was opened in two sections, north of Tiverton in 1884, while the stretch south of Tiverton saw its first passenger trains the following year. The line crossed the River Exe many times, often passing delightfully situated halts surrounded by quaint thatched cottages with picturesque gardens. The line was largely steam-worked before its closure, which occurred on 7th October 1963. Unfortunately, the last trains were diesel-worked, much to the annoyance of some local people who turned out on the last day. Bulk grain to Thorverton continued after closure to passengers, but the rest of the line was shut completely. Tiverton continued to be served by trains from Tiverton Junction until 5th October 1964. *Alan Jarvis*

Left, above: A scene at Barnstaple Junction on 28th September 1963 as Ivatt Class '2MT' 2-6-2T No.41216 pulls out with a train for Torrington. The first section of this line was opened to passengers as far as Fremington in August 1854 and extended to Bideford the following year. A further extension, to Torrington, became operational on 1st July 1872. Torrington remained the limit of the line for more than 50 years, until, in 1925, the North Devon & Cornwall Junction Light Railway opened through to Halwill Junction, using the trackbed of an abandoned narrow gauge line. The line south of Torrington was closed to passengers from 1st March 1965, while the northern end of the line, from Barnstaple to Torrington lost its passenger service seven months later. In January 1968 the Barnstaple to Bideford stretch was temporarily reopened to provide a service across a river after a roadbridge had been damaged. Freight traffic lasted as far as Meeth until the early 1980s.
Alan Jarvis

Left, below: One of the little Midland Railway Johnson-designed Class '2F' 0-6-0s, No.58148, leaves Glenfield tunnel with a Leicester West Bridge branch freight, on 7th December 1963. This was the very last day an engine of this type worked the line, the last three survivors being withdrawn from Coalville shed shortly afterwards. There was a large domestic coal depot at West Bridge and heavy trains operated on the branch, the '2F's being the only class which was allowed to pass through the restricted confines of the 1,796 yards-long Glenfield tunnel. No.58148 dated from 1876 and was originally MR No.2967. This section of line once formed part of the Leicester & Swannington Railway which was opened in 1832 to transport coal from the West Leicestershire coalfield to the city of Leicester. It was the oldest constituent of the MR when that company was formed fourteen years later.
Neville Simms

The Ivatt Class '2MT' 2-6-0s were associated with the Cambrian lines for many years, being ideally suited to the secondary passenger duties which were common in this area. In this view, a shaft of sunlight illuminates No.46521 as it makes a brisk departure from Barmouth with the 9.45am train to Dolgellau, in February 1964. No.46521 emerged from Swindon works in late February 1953 and was initially allocated to Oswestry shed. However, it soon moved to Brecon, in Central Wales, and worked from there to Rhayader, Moat Lane Junction, Three Cocks Junction and Hereford. In October 1959 No.46521 was transferred back to Oswestry and remained there for 3½ years before moving to Machynlleth, from where it worked to Aberystwyth, Pwllheli and Welshpool. During this period it was often seen on Barmouth to Dolgellau trains. After a pathetically short working life of just over 13½ years No.46521 was withdrawn, merely 'surplus to requirements', in November 1966. The engine was despatched to Barry scrapyard and rested there until it was bought for preservation on the Severn Valley Railway, where it arrived on 20th March 1971.

Mike Hudson

The line from Shoreham-by-Sea to Horsham, in West Sussex, was opened in 1861 and for many years was worked by LBSCR locomotive classes on motor trains. In the 1950s LSWR 'M7' Class 0-4-4Ts could be seen on the route, but these later gave way to SECR 'H' Class engines. In March 1961 the 'H' Class was ousted by LMSR Ivatt 2-6-2Ts displaced from the LMR. The line was one of the last in West Sussex to be steam-worked, and when diesel units took over in May 1964 the inevitable closure of Brighton shed soon followed. It is recorded that engine Nos.41294 and 41313 shared the duties on 3rd May 1964, the last day of steam. In this shot, sister engine No.41230 is seen near Old Shoreham heading north with a Brighton to Horsham train on 11th April 1964, during the steam's final full month of operation. The line followed the River Adur for some distance, one of the river's dyked banks being visible on the right.

Mike Hudson

In the summer of 1963 the WR announced that the London to Worcester and Hereford trains, which were the last steam worked main line services from Paddington, would be taken over by diesel traction in September. The 11.10am from Worcester to Paddington on 7th September 1963, hauled by No. 7023 *Penrice Castle*, was expected to be the last steam working from Worcester to the Capital and, according to plan, the return working was powered by a 'Hymek' diesel. But the WR operating authorities had not anticipated the scandalous unreliability of the new diesels, with no fewer than 73 substitutions of steam for diesel traction being recorded in the first three weeks of the new arrangements. In November, the temporary withdrawal of some 'Western'

diesels exacerbated the situation, which became so desperate that even Stanier 'Black Fives' were occasionally commandeered. During the first half of 1964 there was some improvement in diesel availability, and from the beginning of May a determined effort was made to eliminate steam passenger trains from the route. Even this was not wholly successful however, because steam continued to work the Worcester to Hereford section! In this view, taken on 11th April 1964, during the final weeks of regular steam working, No. 7928 *Wolf Hall* is pictured near Old Oak Common with the 3.15pm Paddington to Worcester train.

R. C. Riley

During the early 1960s York-based 'V2' Class 2-6-2s had various overnight freight workings to Woodford Halse, on the former Great Central line. By 1964, however, the class had become less common on the GC route, so the appearance of No.60963 working the 11.15am Nottingham (Victoria) to Marylebone empty newspaper train on 18th April 1964 was, perhaps, surprising. The train was photographed just south of Woodford Halse. It is likely that the V2 was a last-minute replacement for a failed Class '5MT' or 'Royal Scot'. The 'V2' Class first appeared on the GC line in October 1938, when members of the class were shedded at Neasden and Leicester, but they were moved away in the early years of the war. They later reappeared in some strength from the end of 1948, with the largest allocation being based at Woodford Halse, and were allocated to GC sheds until the early 1960s.

Neville Simms

The Great Central Railway's 'O4' Class 2-8-0s, designed by John Robinson, first saw the light of day in 1911 and played a large part in the GCR's 1914-1918 war effort. Their robust design features, simplicity and reliability persuaded the government to adopt the type and batches were constructed under government order for military use during the First World War. The class became very widely travelled, and in addition to working in many parts of Great Britain and Europe, some examples were sold to China and Australia, while others were used in Egypt. After the grouping there were 131 Class 'O4's in LNER service, plus 17 Class 'O5's, the latter being a similar, but later, design of Robinson 2-8-0 with a larger boiler. A further 273 Class 'O4's were purchased by the LNER between 1923 and 1929. The 'O5's were rebuilt from 1924 using an 'O4' boiler and reclassified O4/6. During the ensuing years reboilering, new smokeboxes and cabs, resulted in no fewer than eight sub-divisions of the class being created. Some engines were rebuilt with a standard 100A boiler and double side window cab and reclassified O4/8, including No.63914, seen here shunting at Staveley on 9th May 1964. Interestingly, this machine actually started life as an 'O5' Class, so was rebuilt twice during its career. This engine was withdrawn later that year and, after a long and colourful history, the last representatives of this hugely successful class were condemned in 1966.

Gavin Morrison

On the sunny morning of 20th June 1964, 'Coronation' Pacific No.46254 *City of Stoke-on-Trent* leaves Crewe with the 9.25am Crewe to Aberdeen train. By this time the class had only three months of active use remaining before the survivors were withdrawn *en masse* in September. An unexpected event during the summer of 1964 was the return of steam engines to the working of the down 'Mid-Day Scot' on Sundays. On 5th July No.46254 appeared on this duty, while a fortnight later sister engine No.46250 *City of Lichfield* was noted. A few days after its appearance on the 'Mid-Day Scot' *City of Stoke-on-Trent* was seen passing Preston on a menial freight duty, but had a final fling on express passenger duty when it again worked the down 'Mid-Day Scot' on 30th August. No.46254 was condemned on 12th September and later sold to Cashmores, of Great Bridge, for breaking-up.   *Brian Magilton*

Right, above: Following the introduction of 'Western' diesel-hydraulics (later Class 52) on the Birmingham to Paddington services in September 1962, only the 5.50pm (Fridays only) Birmingham Snow Hill to Paddington remained regularly steam worked. Here this train is pictured approaching Solihull station with a reasonably clean 'Castle' Class 4-6-0 No.7014 *Caerhays Castle* in charge on 3rd July 1964. By the end of 1964, only two booked duties reportedly existed for the eleven 'Castles' remaining in traffic, these being the above train plus the 12.5am (Sundays only) Manchester to Plymouth, which was 'Castle'-hauled between Wolverhampton Low Level and Bristol via Worcester. *Michael Mensing*

Right, below: The final years of steam traction were noteworthy for a number of unprecedented locomotive workings, with engines sometimes straying many miles from their normal haunts. One of the most remarkable workings took place on 9th October 1963 when an 'A4' Class Pacific reached Derby on a passenger train. On 15th August 1964 a 'Grange' 4-6-0 worked as far as Huddersfield, apparently due to a derailment the previous day on the WR, which resulted in a number of dislocated engine workings. In the south, one of the highlights of 1964 was the visit of 'B1' Class 4-6-0 No.61313, which powered a pigeon special to Lewes in June and later failed at Eastbourne shed. It left Eastbourne on 6th July, travelling at slow speed to Redhill for repairs. The interloper's sojourn at Redhill lasted for some months and on 1st/2nd October the 'B1' was put to work on passenger duties to Reading. It eventually left the SR on 3rd October. Another visitor to Redhill shed at this time was Class '5MT' No.44951 which was also 'stopped' for repair, after failing at Haywards Heath on a Newcastle to Newhaven car-sleeper. The strangers are seen in this shot taken at Redhill shed on 10th July, with GWR 4-6-0 No.7808 *Cookham Manor*, which had hauled a regular working from Reading, plus a local 'Q' Class 0-6-0 and BR Standard 2-6-4T. *David Clark*

A badly-leaking LMSR 'Royal Scot' Class 4-6-0, No.46155 *The Lancer* is seen on the 'East Lancs' side of Preston station with a Glasgow to Blackpool train, which also conveyed a Southport portion, which would be taken forward from Preston by a 2-6-4T locomotive. The train is facing south and is about to proceed along the East Lancs line, before rejoining the West Coast main line at Farington Curve Junction. This detour was often undertaken by summer holiday trains in order to avoid operationally inconvenient reversals in Preston station. This picture was taken on 15th August 1964, a year which saw a total of twenty-one 'Royal Scots' condemned, including the example seen here, which was withdrawn in December. This part of Preston station was closed in 1972 and has since been redeveloped.

Brian Magilton

Bescot shed was the last to use the LNWR 'Super D' 0-8-0s, a distinctive design dating from the turn of the century. The name 'Super D' is derived from the fact that these engines were a superheated version of the LNWR 'D' Class. In the early 1960s they were to be found in large numbers in the north-west, particularly at Wigan, Edge Hill and Buxton, but by 1964 the class had been reduced to a small pocket working from Bescot. Some members of the class were fitted with a tender cab, which made life more comfortable for the enginemen when working tender first. The locomotive depicted here is No.49407, which is assisting Class '5MT' No.44873 on a freight train at Pleck Junction, in Walsall, on 21st August 1964. Walsall gasworks, where a Peckett shunter is partially visible, is on the left, while the industrial landscape of the West Midlands forms the backdrop. The final workings of the class took place on 24th December 1964, on which date Nos.49361 and 49430 were laid aside. *Peter Fitton*

More than 400 of these Class '3F' 0-6-0Ts – commonly known as 'Jinties'– were built between 1924 and 1930 and they became the standard LMSR shunting engine, being an everyday sight throughout the system, apart from Scotland. They were the Fowler post-grouping development of the Johnson Midland Railway design. This example, No.47662, seen here shunting at Carnforth on 26th August 1964, was built in March 1929 and remained in service until January 1966. The last 'Jinties' in BR stock were retained at Westhouses shed, in Derbyshire, to shunt at Williamthorpe Colliery. In August 1967 three locomotives, Nos.47289, 47383 and 47629, assisted by 'J94' Class 0-6-0ST No.68012, were in use at the pit. Two engines were required in traffic at a time and they reportedly worked twenty-four hours a day on a twenty-five day roster. They regularly double-headed a loaded coal train from the washing plant to the main line. The 'Jinties', and the 'J94' locomotive, were the last standard gauge tank engines on BR, when they were replaced by NCB diesels on 6th October 1967.

Gavin Morrison

The LSWR ran an 11.0am train from Waterloo to the West Country as long ago as 1890 and it was not until 1926 that it became known as the 'Atlantic Coast Express'. The name was chosen as a result of a competition amongst Southern Railway staff. During the summer service period, the 11.0am train served Ilfracombe, Torrington and Plymouth while a second train, which left London ten minutes later, carried the same title, and conveyed portions to Bude, Padstow and East Devon. The 'ACE', as it was known, became the most multi-portioned train in the country, one of its most noticeable features being the preponderance of brake composite coaches, which were necessary for the various portions. In the summer of 1952 substantial accelerations occurred and these included the Southern's first mile-a-minute schedule. By 1961 the 'ACE' was booked to cover the 83¾ mile Waterloo to Salisbury section in 80 minutes. In 1963 the Western Region took control west of Salisbury and downgrading of the route to secondary status soon followed. The weekday 'ACE', which was on a faster schedule than the Saturday train, ran for the last time on 4th September 1964 and here spotless 'Merchant Navy' Pacific No. 35022 *Holland America Line* is depicted waiting to leave Waterloo on that date.

John Phillips

When administration of the Salisbury to Exeter line was transferred to the Western Region it was soon reduced to secondary line status. From 7th September 1964 the WR introduced a 'Warship' diesel-hauled semi-fast service between Waterloo and Exeter St Davids only, and through carriages to points beyond Exeter were withdrawn. On 5th September 1964, the last Saturday of regular steam working west of Salisbury, BR Standard Class '5MT' No.73162 is depicted leaving Honiton tunnel with an unidentified up express. The changes made by the WR, which included closure of stations and partial singling of the track, were seen by many observers as being too draconian, and happily since that time the line has witnessed a considerable revival. *Roy Hobbs*

LNER Pacific No.60036 *Colombo*, pictured on stand-by duty at Darlington shed on 26th September 1964, was one of 78 'A3' Class engines, the vast majority of which spent their careers on the East Coast main line. No.60036 was constructed as No.2501 at Doncaster Works in July 1934 and became BR No.60036 in July 1948. In November 1958 it was equipped with a double chimney and received trough smoke deflectors in July 1962. By the time of this picture, the fortunes of this famous class were at a low ebb, because regular express passenger steam workings were a thing of the past on the East Coast route, and only a handful of these thoroughbreds remained. The last main line steam passenger working in the north-east was the 4.30pm Newcastle to Berwick, which usually produced an 'A1' or 'A3' Class Pacific or 'V2' 2-6-2. In the mid-1960s the surviving LNER Pacifics eked out an insecure existence on seasonal workings or deputising for diesels. On 12th November 1964 No.60112 *St. Simon* became the very last 'A3' to work on the southern section of the GN main line when it reportedly powered an empty coaching stock train as far as Hornsey. *Colombo* was withdrawn in November 1964, and by the end of that year the 'A3' class was reduced to three members, all allocated to the Scottish Region.

Mike Hudson

The push-pull auto train was as much a part of Great Western tradition as 'Kings' and 'Castles' and this service was among the last to operate. It ran from Gloucester Central to Chalford, the latter station being located at the eastern end of the beautiful Golden Valley, on the main line to Swindon. The auto trains sprinted along the first nine miles from Gloucester to Stonehouse, running alongside the Midland main line to Bristol for most of the way. But after leaving Stonehouse there were no fewer than ten stops in the seven miles to Chalford, including Stroud, which was by far the busiest station served by the 'Chalford Flyer', as it was known locally. In this picture, which is enhanced by the first of the autumn tints on the trees bordering the track, '14XX' Class 0-4-2T No.1458 is seen approaching Chalford with a train from Gloucester on 6th October 1964. The service was withdrawn just over three weeks later, when all of the smaller stations and halts were closed.   *R. C. Riley*

The attractive Gloucester to Hereford branch turned off the main line from Gloucester to Severn Tunnel Junction at Grange Court Junction and passed through some outstandingly beautiful countryside. It provided one of the most pleasant and relaxing journeys one could wish for. Unfortunately, apart from the historic town of Ross-on-Wye, the line served no major centres of population, which proved its undoing, closure taking place on 31st October 1964. Between Grange Court and Ross-on-Wye, the line skirted the Forest of Dean, while the northern section of the line crossed and re-crossed the meandering River Wye. Here, Churchward 'Mogul' No.7318 is depicted leaving the isolated station of Mitcheldean Road with a Hereford-bound train in October 1964, during the last few weeks of the line's existence.

John Phillips

The rapid decline of steam traction in the 1960s caused an upsurge of interest in steam railways, which was manifested in the increasing number of railtours being operated. Tours were usually run over routes facing closure or to provide a last opportunity for a journey behind locomotives scheduled for early withdrawal. Societies vied with each other to produce the most innovative itinerary or unusual motive power. On 18th October 1964 two of the most prominent societies in this field, the RCTS and LCGB, joined forces to run 'The Midhurst Belle', which was the last train to traverse the Pulborough to Midhurst branch, in West Sussex. Locomotives used on this train included a 'USA' Class tank engine, from Guildford to Horsham, and Maunsell 'Q' Class 0-6-0 No.30530 from Horsham to Midhurst, the latter continuing on to Littlehampton. The use of steam traction to and from Littlehampton, where steam on passenger trains was very rare, was interesting enough, but the choice of a 'Merchant Navy' Pacific for the run along the coast to Preston Park, must have been one of the reasons why the tour was oversubscribed! Here, No.35007 *Aberdeen Commonwealth* is depicted leaving Littlehampton *en route* to Preston Park, where the train reversed in order to enter Brighton station. The tour later visited the Kemp Town branch and the, hopefully contented, participants rounded off the day with an excellent run from Brighton to Victoria behind No.35007.

John Phillips

The first withdrawals of Sir Nigel Gresley's legendary 'A4' Class Pacifics occurred in December 1962, when five examples based at Kings Cross, including the record-breaking No.60014 *Silver Link*, were condemned. In June 1963 Kings Cross shed was closed and steam traction was completely banned, at least in theory(!), south of Hitchin, the eleven remaining 'A4's at Kings Cross being transferred to Peterborough. In October 1963 a further five 'A4's were withdrawn, the remainder being sent to the Scottish Region. Despite the official ban on steam at the southern end of the GN main line, the chronic unreliability of the diesel fleet resulted in many appearances of steam locomotives at Kings Cross, no fewer than 40 being recorded in December 1963 alone. The last recorded working of an 'A4' from Kings Cross in ordinary traffic was that of No. 60017 *Silver Fox* on the 6.40pm to Leeds on 29th October 1963, a mere nine

days after the engine's official withdrawal! In June 1964 the last 'A4's in England, Nos.60001/2/20, were taken out of service at Gateshead. The RCTS/SLS organised a railtour, from Kings Cross to Newcastle and return, to mark the sad end of these machines on the East Coast main line. The ten-coach train, which ran on 24th October 1964, was hauled by No.60009 *Union of South Africa* which covered the 27 miles from Hitchin to Huntingdon at an average speed of 83mph, but unfortunately a broken rail at High Dyke spoiled the remainder of the down run. On the return trip No.60009 ran like an engine possessed, with 100mph being registered on the engine's speedometer near Essendine, and the train reached London half-an-hour early. In this shot *Union of South Africa*, which is now preserved, is seen at Gateshead shed prior to returning to Kings Cross.

Ken Groundwater

The end of October 1964 saw the withdrawal of passenger trains from a number of branches in Gloucestershire, including the Berkeley Road to Sharpness service. Sharpness, on the east bank of the River Severn, was the principal station of the Severn & Wye Joint Railway, which was operated by the GWR and Midland companies. The service originally ran across the river to Lydney, but during the late evening of 25th October 1960 two barges collided with one of the piers of the railway bridge in thick fog, demolishing two spans.

Initially, there was some optimism that repairs to the bridge would be undertaken, but these hopes proved to be unfounded and the passenger service on the surviving remnant of the line, from Berkeley Road to Sharpness, was left to wither away. Here, the 8.15am from Berkeley Road, with '14XX' Class 0-4-2T No.1453 in charge, is pictured awaiting departure to Sharpness on 31st October 1964, the last day of passenger services. *Hugh Ballantyne*

The Redhill to Reading line opened in 1849, and initially there were four weekday trains on the route, the fastest of these taking just under two hours for the 47 miles. The section between Guildford and Redhill ran along the foot of the North Downs and was particularly scenic, offering superb views. For many years the route was the preserve of various SECR 4-4-0 classes, but these gave way to Maunsell 'Moguls' in the 1950s. During the summer months, until 1962, the route was used extensively by holiday trains from the Midlands to South Coast resorts, these sometimes being worked by GWR 2-6-0s or 'Manor' Class 4-6-0s. Dieselisation of the line, using hybrid three-car units, took place on Monday 4th January 1965 and it was appropriate that Maunsell engines, which had a long association with the route, virtually monopolised services during the final weekend. Locomotives used included 'N' Class 'Mogul' No.31862, which is depicted leaving Betchworth with a Reading train on the last day of regular steam. The siding on the left served the Betchworth Greystone Lime Co., which owned a fleet of unique industrial engines.

Roy Hobbs

Like other LNER Pacific Classes, the last working 'A3's were to be found in Scotland. The class became extinct in England in late 1964, which left three 'A3's north of the border – Nos.60041 *Salmon Trout*, 60052 *Prince Palatine* and 60100 *Spearmint*. This trio was normally to be found on Waverley route freights and could occasionally be observed double-heading on especially heavy trains. On 19th February 1965, No.60052 was seen paired with 'V2' No.60835 on a Milford Haven to Thornton additional block oil working – what a rousing sight and sound that must have been! On 26th April No.60041 was piloted by a 'B1' Class on a Bathgate to Ditton Junction train of empty carflats.

Spearmint fell by the wayside in June, but the other two remained at work and sometimes turned up on passenger workings, one notable sighting being that of *Prince Palatine*, which hauled the 7.45pm Aberdeen to Edinburgh on 27th August. *Salmon Trout* was condemned in November 1965, while *Prince Palatine* was officially withdrawn in January 1966. The unpredictable movements of the three survivors ensured that they would be rarely photographed, but No.60100 *Spearmint* was recorded passing the closed Falkland Road station, in Fife, with an up train of empty coaching stock, on 16th April 1965, shortly before its demise.   *K.M. Falconer*

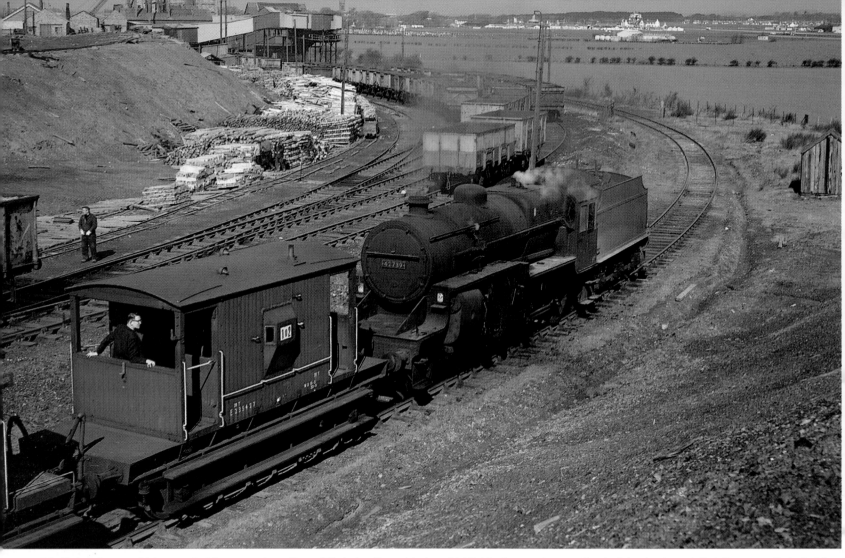

Of all the classes which operated in some strength on BR during the period covered by this book, it was photographs of the LMSR Class '5P4F' 'Moguls', commonly known as 'Crabs', which proved by far the most elusive. This picture features a very dirty No.42739, which is seen posing for cameras at Glenburn colliery, near Prestwick, Ayrshire, during the course of the 'Scottish Rambler No.4' railtour on 16th April 1965. Presumably the tour included a brake van trip along the colliery branch. The 'Scottish Rambler' tours, which were the highlight of some steam enthusiasts' calendars at that time, usually lasted four days over the Easter Bank Holiday period, and took participants over many obscure routes in areas where steam traction was still available. The 'Crabs', of which 245 were constructed between 1926 and 1932, were robust and workmanlike machines, the last of them not being withdrawn until 1967. Some examples have fortunately survived into preservation.

Chris Gammell

A Glasgow to Gourock train, headed by an unidentified Fairburn 2-6-4T, passes Blackstone Junction, west of Paisley, on 17th April 1965. Note the varied selection of non-corridor coaches forming the train. At this date, steam traction still had just over two years of use remaining on the Glasgow suburban services to Gourock and Wemyss Bay, for which an electrification scheme had been approved. The last regular steam workings on these routes from Glasgow Central took place on 28th April 1967, when Class '5MT' No.44699 took the 6.55am to Hillington West and BR Standard 2-6-4T No.80004 hauled the 7.19am to Renfrew. But the final working, the 5.3pm from Gourock to Glasgow, was appropriately hauled by Fairburn 2-6-4T No.42274, a class which had a long association with the area. It had latterly been employed as a Beattock banker and had appeared at Polmadie only a few days previously. With the notable exception of two veteran 'J36' Class 0-6-0s, which were apparently retained for possible use in a film(!), all remaining ScR steam engines were withdrawn from 1st May 1967. However, one or two LMR diagrams continued to bring steam across the border, the 8.32pm Carlisle to Perth passenger train becoming the last booked steam passenger train in Scotland, although even that finished a month later. *Chris Gammell*

The first railway in Galloway, south west Scotland, was the line connecting Dumfries and Castle Douglas which opened in 1859. This line was still being built when an extension westwards to Stranraer and Portpatrick was authorised. There had been a more or less regular sailing from Portpatrick to Donaghadee for many years and the line's promoters almost certainly had an eye on the Irish traffic. Stranraer was reached in 1861, but the opposition of local landowners resulted in wide detours being made which often meant that stations were on the fringe of their towns, or, in the cases of Gatehouse of Fleet and New Galloway, some miles distant. In 1885 the section from Castle Douglas to Portpatrick, became the Portpatrick and Wigtownshire Joint Railway, which in turn became part of the LMSR at the grouping. This view shows BR Standard Class '4MT' 2-6-4T No.80061 at Newton Stewart on 29th May 1965.

Chris Gammell

A beautiful picture of a train in the landscape near Newton Stewart on 29th May 1965. Unfortunately, precise details are unknown, but it is likely that the train is the afternoon 'stopper' from Stranraer to Dumfries with BR Standard tank engine No.80061 in charge. The Dumfries to Stranraer line, or 'Port Road' as it was known, traversed a wild and desolate area with limited potential for the railway. Most of the traffic was concentrated at the eastern end of the line, between Dumfries, Castle Douglas and Kirkcudbright. Prior to closure, the main 30 mile-long section of the route from Castle Douglas to Newton Stewart was served by only three trains a day and one of those was 'The Northern Irishman', an overnight boat train to and from London, which often required double-heading over the line's stiff gradients. A curious situation existed at Gatehouse of Fleet station, which, in the 1963 summer timetable, only had three trains per week to Stranraer, on Mondays, Fridays and Saturdays, but no service in the opposite direction! Sadly, the 'Port Road', which passed through one of the most remote areas of Scotland, was closed in June 1965.

Chris Gammell

One of the last steam turns from Radyr shed was a daily trip working to a dolomite quarry, which was situated on a hillside at Taffs Well, north of Cardiff. Dolomite is a mineral used for lining blast furnaces. The quarry was served from Penrhos Junction by a former Barry Railway main line which was originally built to tap the coal resources of the Monmouthshire valleys, albeit by the time of the picture only this section remained. The photographer had obtained a lift in the brake van and this picture, taken on 4th June 1965, shows the train on the famous viaduct at Taffs Well, with the quarry partially visible in the background. Radyr, the last steam shed in the Cardiff valleys, was shut on 24th July 1965, and its closure marked the complete dieselisation of the area.

Alan Jarvis

'Castle' Class 4-6-0 No. 7029 *Clun Castle* pulls out of Paddington on 11th June 1965 with the very last scheduled steam-hauled passenger train from the terminus, the 4.15pm to Banbury. No. 7029 was one of four 'Castles' nominally in traffic on this date, though this total included No. 7022 *Hereford Castle* stored at Gloucester. At the end of June however, three of the remaining engines were withdrawn, leaving *Clun Castle* as the sole survivor. During July it was noted on the 5.45am Gloucester to Cardiff train, in addition to powering several freight and departmental workings in the Gloucester area. No. 7029 spent much of September in Worcester Works receiving attention to its pistons and valve gear, but was back in the public eye when it was displayed at Bristol Bath Road open day on 23rd October. On numerous occasions during December it was on station pilot duty at Gloucester Central and sometimes worked the 5.0pm local train from there to Cheltenham. It worked this train for the last time on 31st December and was withdrawn on the following day.

R.C. Riley

The closure of the Eastbourne to Tunbridge Wells 'Cuckoo' line and the Horsham to Guildford route from 14th June 1965 resulted in the virtual elimination of steam traction from the SR's Central Division, and the division's remaining steam sheds were officially closed from the same date. To mark this melancholy occasion the Locomotive Club of Great Britain arranged 'The Wealdsman' railtour for Sunday 13th June. In addition to the above-mentioned routes, the tour also included the Three Bridges to East Grinstead and Shoreham to Horsham lines, both of which were threatened with the Beeching axe at that time, and were subsequently closed. The Horsham to Guildford line had always been a sleepy backwater with a sparse service, so it was, perhaps, surprising it had escaped closure for so long. The line had no Sunday service, so this tour, seen here leaving Baynards behind a pair of 'Q1'Class 0-6-0s, Nos.33027 and 33006, was the very last working to traverse the route. Baynards station was in an isolated location, being built solely to serve a nearby country estate.

John Phillips

Many relatively new steam classes were sacrificed as a result of BR's doctrinaire dieselisation policies, and hundreds of modern locomotives in excellent condition were scrapped long before they were life-expired. The Peppercorn 'A1' Class Pacifics, introduced in 1948, were a typical case and dieselisation resulted in these engines having an average life of only fifteen years. Withdrawal commenced in the autumn of 1962 with a total of six engines being withdrawn in that year. A similar number were condemned in 1963, while in 1964 eleven went for scrap. In 1965, no fewer than 24 were withdrawn, leaving only Nos.60124 *Kenilworth* and 60145 *Saint Mungo* at work in 1966. Prior to the diesel invasion, the 'A1's were used on front-line express work on the East Coast main line, and were particularly associated with the Kings Cross-Leeds services. In the twilight of their short careers they could be found on a variety of mundane tasks, including working freight and van trains. During the summer of 1964 they made occasional sorties over the Settle and Carlisle line. The example seen here is No.60154 (formerly *Bon Accord*) which was photographed at York while working the 8.45am Leeds to Glasgow train on 10th July 1965. Built in April 1951, No.60154 had a tragically brief working life, being withdrawn three months after this picture was taken. *Mike Hudson*

The summer of 1965 saw the end of steam traction on holiday expresses from Wolverhampton Low Level to the West of England via the Honeybourne line, which were steam worked as far as Bristol. There was a tiny handful of turns, and some of the trains were worked by BR Standard 'Britannia' Pacifics, three of which, Nos.70045, 70047 and 70053, were based at Oxley at that time. LMSR and BR Class '5MT' 4-6-0s were also observed. GWR motive power was still in evidence, for instance on 31st July No.6855 *Saighton Grange* was turned out to haul the 6.55am Wolverhampton to Penzance, returning on the

12.30pm Penzance to Wolverhampton, which is pictured between Wickwar and Charfield. In addition to being in deplorable external condition, the locomotive was also without name or numberplates. It was soon put out of its misery however, being condemned a little over two months later. Following a suggestion by the Cheltenham branch of the RCTS to BR, Bristol, *Clun Castle* worked this train on 4th September, thus providing a fitting climax to the 1965 summer timetable, which proved to be the last season of steam-worked holiday trains from the West Midlands to the South West.   *Michael Mensing*

LMSR Class '6P' 'Royal Scot' No.46115 *Scots Guardsman* makes a spirited departure from Carstairs, on 31st July 1965, with the 1.12pm relief train from Liverpool to Glasgow. Only five 'Royal Scots' lasted into 1965 and by the time of this photograph only two, Nos.46115 and 46140, remained in stock. During the last months of its career No.46115 appears to have been reasonably active. A fortnight prior to this picture, on 17th July, it was most unusually noted on the Waverley route, working the 9.50am Saturdays only train from Edinburgh Waverley to Sheffield. On 4th August it worked a Carlisle to Margam freight to Chester, while in September it powered a special to Blackpool. On 9th October No.46115 was noted passing Preston with an up freight and on 20th October it hauled the 4.45pm Glasgow St Enoch to Carlisle parcels train. But on 5th November *Scots Guardsman* was noted under repair at Carlisle Kingmoor shed and was withdrawn the following month. Fortunately, No.46115 was rescued for preservation and made an appearance on the main line some years ago, but has since maintained a low profile.

K. M. Falconer

One of Dundee (Tay Bridge) shed's Class 'A2' Pacifics had a rare outing on express passenger duty on 30th August 1965, when No.60530 *Sayajirao* worked the 10.0am from Dundee to Glasgow and is seen approaching Hilton tunnel, soon after leaving Perth, in fine style. It returned to Dundee later in the day at the head of the 6.15pm ex-Glasgow. The Pacific was turned out especially to work these trains on this day, apparently as a favour for an enthusiast who had supplied the ScR with publicity photographs. *Sayajirao* was normally confined to freight or stand-by duties, so its activities were completely unpredictable. During 1965, it was reported working an Aberdeen to Perth freight on 23rd January, while six days later it hauled a Millerhill to Carlisle freight over the Waverley route. In July it worked a train of empty stock from Aberdeen to Edinburgh. Built at Doncaster in March 1948, No.60530 was withdrawn from service in November 1966.

Derek Penney

Gresley's 'V2' class 2-6-2s have been described as 'the engines that won the war' – at least for the LNER! This may have been something of an over-statement, but they were undoubtedly one of their designer's best and most successful classes. In wartime they were noted for their prodigious haulage capacity, which is illustrated by the remarkable feat of No.4800, which hauled a 26-coach, 860 tons, load from Peterborough to Kings Cross on 31st March 1940. It is recorded that only nine minutes were booked against the engine. In all 184 locomotives were built, 159 at Darlington Works and the remainder at Doncaster. 'V2's were allocated to Scottish sheds when new and by the end of 1938 four machines were based at Dundee, with a similar total at Aberdeen (Ferryhill) so the class became a common sight on East Coast main line mixed traffic duties. They later worked express passenger trains along the LMSR's

Perth to Kinnaber Junction 'Strathmore' route, and by 1956 were rostered for the 3.30pm Aberdeen to Euston 'West Coast Postal'. By the mid-1960s the 'V2's had been decimated by withdrawals and only fourteen examples survived into 1966, of which nine were based in Scotland, at Dundee and Edinburgh (St. Margarets) sheds. They were used on a variety of work, including summer Saturday passenger trains, such as the 9.13am Dundee to Blackpool, as far as Edinburgh. Most of the remaining engines were withdrawn at the end of the summer, leaving only No.60836 to soldier on until December, by which time it had gained the considerable distinction of being the last active member of its class. No.60973, seen here shunting at Perth in September 1965, was also one of the few engines which survived until 1966.

Derek Penney

The era of steam-worked push-pull trains on BR came to an end when the last-remaining service, from Seaton to Stamford, was replaced by diesel railcars from 4th October 1965. Closure of the shed at Market Harborough, which normally supplied motive power for the service, was effected from the same date. For some time the branch had been the preserve of BR Standard Class '2MT' 2-6-2Ts, but Ivatt 2-6-2Ts took over some weeks prior to closure, Nos.41212 or 41219 usually being rostered. Here, on a wet 16th September 1965, No.41212 is seen at Stamford shortly after arrival with the 9.35am from Seaton. The end of steam on this quiet rural line sealed the fate of the two 'Ivatts', both of which were condemned in the following month.

Hugh Ballantyne

GWR steam on the Cambrian main line from Shrewsbury to Aberystwyth came to an end during the autumn of 1965, when the last 'Manor' 4-6-0s were withdrawn from Shrewsbury shed. In this photograph, No.7812 *Erlestoke Manor* is seen climbing Talerddig bank with the up 'Cambrian Coast Express' on 20th September 1965. By this date the era of immaculately turned out 'Manors' on this train was over, and with No.7812's demise imminent, it was not surprisingly looking a trifle neglected. The locomotive was also running without nameplates. During the summer of 1965 the principal duties of Shrewsbury's 'Manors' were the overnight Crewe to Aberystwyth mail train plus the 'Cambrian Coast Express'. When the last Collett 0-6-0 was withdrawn in May, the 'Manors' became the sole GWR class active on the route, the remaining steam services being largely in the hands of BR Standard Class '4MT' tender engines. Thanks to the efforts of preservationists, *Erlestoke Manor* was saved and, at the time of writing, can be seen at Swindon.

Neville Simms

Few railways can have been so full of charm and character as the Somerset and Dorset line, which was created in 1862 as a result of the amalgamation of the Somerset Central and Dorset Central companies. At that time the S&D ran from Burnham-on-Sea, in Somerset, to Wimborne, in Dorset, twelve years elapsing before the steeply graded Bath Extension was opened. Construction of the extension over the Mendip Hills brought total financial exhaustion to the S&D company, which was then leased jointly to the Midland Railway and LSWR. The route's heyday was probably after the Second World War, when the line carried intense summer Saturday holiday traffic from the Midlands and north of England. On peak days virtually every serviceable engine was pressed into traffic and this resulted in some remarkable locomotive combinations, for which the S&D was renowned. In September 1962, the holiday trains were diverted away from the S&D, the route then being reduced in status to little more than a branch line. It subsequently died a lingering death, being slowly strangled at the hands of the Western Region. The S&D was tabled for closure in the Beeching Report and – after an agonisingly long wait – closure was sanctioned by the government to take place in early January 1966, although this was later deferred for two months. This view shows the 1.10pm Bournemouth to Bristol train, hauled by BR Standard Class '4MT' No. 76009 entering Sturminster Newton on 13th November 1965.

Bill Chapman

When the 'Pines Express' and other inter-regional services were diverted away from the Somerset & Dorset line in 1962, it was clear that BR was determined to close the line. The 1963 timetable still included stopping trains which had connected with the 'Pines Express' in the previous timetable. This was apparently part of a deliberate policy aimed at making the S&D as uneconomic as possible, in order to strengthen the case for closure. At the same time, the WR was diverting as much goods traffic as possible away from the S&D, and in 1964 all night freight traffic was withdrawn. In September 1965, the inevitable closure of the line was announced, and the date fixed for 3rd January 1966. In the event there were problems with granting licences for the replacement buses, and the closure was postponed, much to the embarrassment of the Western Region, which had already announced that steam was to be eliminated from the region from that date. A much-reduced 'emergency' service was introduced and this operated until early March. So, in the end, the 'serene and delightful' Somerset and Dorset line had been 'sabotaged and defeated'. Here, on 5th March 1966, the last day of public services, '8F' Class 2-8-0 No.48760 is seen approaching Masbury Summit, with the 8.15am Bath to Templecombe local train.   *Neville Simms*

A 1930s or a 1960s scene? GWR 0-6-2T No.6697 struggles up the gradient from Croes Newydd (Wrexham) to Brymbo during a blizzard on 3rd April 1966. The locomotive worked an SLS farewell railtour to the class on 27th March and had '6697' painted on its buffer beam prior to this event. The photographer had been told at Croes Newydd shed that No.6697 was booked to bank a train up to Brymbo, so he must have been very pleasantly surprised to obtain this dramatic shot of it hauling a rake of coke wagons, rather than banking. Two '5600' Class engines, Nos.5605 and 6697, which were usually employed on banking duties, were amongst a tiny pocket of GWR power which survived at Wrexham well into 1966; both were eventually withdrawn in May of that year. In addition, GWR steam lingered at former WR sheds in the West Midlands which were by this time under LMR control, the last examples being withdrawn from Tyseley depot in November 1966. Ironically, GWR steam devotees had to travel to the LMR to see the last working GWR locomotives, the WR's own fleet having been completely withdrawn by the end of 1965.

Derek Huntriss/Colour-Rail

In September 1964 the electrification of the Bournemouth line was announced, the £15m scheme foreshadowing the elimination of steam traction from the Southern Region. The start of electrification work often meant that the main line was closed at night and from January 1965 a regular programme of nightime diversions was operated, from Brookwood to Winchester via Alton and the Mid-Hants line. From April 1966 weekend daytime diversions were also introduced and, although a number of diesels appeared, the majority of trains were steam worked. The Mid-Hants route had been worked by diesel units since 1957, so the sudden appearance of a large number of steam trains on this steeply graded line proved an irresistible attraction to enthusiasts. An additional bonus was the fact that a few of the heaviest trains were double-headed and on one occasion a BR Standard Class '5MT' was noted piloting a Bulleid Pacific. One of the busiest days for diversions was 1st May 1966, and this view shows Bulleid 'West Country' Pacific No.34019 *Bideford* climbing Medstead bank with the 4.30pm from Waterloo to Weymouth. It is still possible to photograph steam trains at this spot, which is now part of the Mid-Hants Railway.

Roger Merry-Price

Three routes originally served the small city of Brechin, a short branch to Edzell, the line to Forfar via Careston and a branch to Bridge of Dun, on the Perth to Aberdeen main line. Had it not been for feuds between the various railway companies in the 1840s, the main Perth to Aberdeen line would probably have been routed via Brechin, one of the major settlements in the area, rather than by-passing the city. The Edzell branch was closed as long ago as 1931, while the Forfar line, which traversed a thinly inhabited area, was shut on 4th August 1952. The line to Bridge of Dun was also closed to passengers on the latter date, but remained open for freight traffic. The rich soil in the Brechin area made it good farming country, and much agricultural traffic was carried, particularly seed potatoes during the season. The branch remained steam worked until 7th April 1967, using North British Railway 'J37' Class 0-6-0s from Dundee (Tay Bridge) shed, which were usually sub-shedded at Montrose between duties. In this picture, No.64577 is depicted shunting at Brechin in May 1966. Despite its early closure to passengers, the attractive station at Brechin remained largely intact and has been taken over by a preservation society, which operates to Bridge of Dun.   *Roy Hobbs*

No book about the run-down of BR steam would be complete without at least one photograph of a WD 'Austerity' Class 2-8-0, the unsung, unglamourous workhorses of heavy freight haulage. The class, which eventually numbered 935 (of which 733 came into BR ownership) was designed by R.A. Riddles for the Ministry of Supply during the Second World War and after the end of hostilities was used on all BR regions at various times, including the SR for a brief period. These engines was especially associated with the mining areas of industrial Lancashire and Yorkshire. Only a handful were based in Scotland, for use on the Fife coal trains, and in the year 1964 these were allocated to Thornton Junction and Dunfermline sheds; Grangemouth also had a small number. In this shot No.90547 is seen powering a coal train from Alloa to Kincardine power station on 28th May 1966. It was just the kind of thankless task that the class performed day in, day out. No.90547 began life at Vulcan Foundry as WD No.77078 and initially worked from Stratford shed, in east London, before moving to March, and later, Neasden. It went to France in 1945, only to return in July of the following year and was stored at Blisworth prior to starting its BR career. The WDs would not have been expected to top a popularity poll amongst steam fans, so consequently no members of this once numerous BR class passed into preservation. This serious omission was later rectified when an example was rescued from Sweden. *Roy Hobbs*

Thirty-five of these Gresley-designed 'J38' Class 0-6-0s were constructed at Darlington works, all within the first five months of 1926. The entire class was earmarked for Scotland and the locomotives were allocated to only four sheds for heavy mineral haulage, in the Fife and Lothian coalfields. The class was one of the last LNER types to remain intact and later became the final Gresley-designed class in traffic. 'J38's were very rarely employed on passenger work. In this view, taken on 28th May 1966, No.65918 is seen approaching Alloa on an empty coal train from Kincardine power station – just the type of work the class undertook quietly and efficiently for decades. Two members of the class survived until April 1967 – the penultimate month of ScR steam.   *Roy Hobbs*

LMSR Class '5MT' No.44941 leaves Loughborough Central, on the Great Central line, with the 6.15pm Nottingham Victoria to Rugby Central train on 8th June 1966. By the time of this photograph, much of the route had already been approved for closure from 5th September 1966. The section from Nottingham to Rugby (including Loughborough) was temporarily reprieved by the Minister of Transport however, and a dmu service continued to operate until May 1969. The stretch of line seen here was later purchased for preservation and today looks totally different to the scene portrayed here.

Services have been progressively extended since trains started to operate again in the mid-1970s and it is possible to travel from Loughborough to Leicester on the GCR route once more, although services now terminate at a new station on the northern fringe of Leicester. One of the original route's claims to fame was that on 3rd September 1966 it carried the 10.45pm (SO) Marylebone to Manchester train, hauled by No.44984, which was the last ordinary service to leave London for the north. *Bill Chapman*

The three-mile long Alnmouth to Alnwick branch of the York, Newcastle & Berwick Railway opened on 19th August 1850, and passed through delightful rural countryside. In 1882, the North Eastern Railway obtained the go-ahead for a line from Alnwick to Coldstream via Wooler, and this opened on 5th September 1887. At the same time a splendid new station was opened at Alnwick, designed by William Bell whose design is purported to have been based on Hull Paragon. The building's most impressive feature was the magnificent overall roof. The station's size was hardly justified by the traffic and it was probably built with an eye to possible Royal visits to nearby Alnwick Castle, home of the Dukes of Northumberland. For many years the branch was worked by NER 4-4-0s, based at Alnmouth shed. The last of these veterans

was withdrawn in 1957, with 'J39' Class 0-6-0s, and to a lesser extent, Gresley 2-6-2Ts, taking over. When the 'J39's left the scene in 1962, 'K1' Class 2-6-0s were drafted in, and these remained staple power on the line until diesel units took over in June 1966. Two unaccustomed classes appeared at the end of steam's career on the branch, these being the visits of Dundee-based 'V2' Class No.60836 in the spring of 1966 and spruced-up '9F' No.92099, which hauled afternoon trains on the final day of steam, 18th June 1966. In this view 'K1' No.62011 is seen with an Alnmouth-bound train on the same day. Closure to passengers occurred in January 1968 and freight facilities were withdrawn in October of the same year.   *Roy Hobbs*

Left, above: In this superbly atmospheric picture, taken in June 1966, 'Castle' Class 4-6-0 No.7029 *Clun Castle* is seen moving onto the turntable inside the roundhouse at Tyseley shed. By this time No.7029 had been officially withdrawn by BR and purchased for private preservation by a trust organised by the late Mr P. B. Whitehouse, the well-known author and photographer. In May and June 1966 *Clun Castle*, although privately owned, was employed on freight trains between Bordesley and Banbury, though reports suggest it was not in the best of condition at that time.   *Derek Huntriss*

Left, below: In the spring of 1962, the Scottish Region announced a whole string of improvements to passenger services, including accelerated Glasgow to Aberdeen trains. At this time steam traction throughout the country was being speedily replaced and enthusiasts were doubtless dumb-founded when it emerged that, not only was steam traction to be employed on the Aberdeen run, but the classes selected were LNER Gresley Pacifics, which were alien to this LMSR route. A test run in February 1962 had established the suitability of these engines and a reshuffle of motive power was decreed which saw 'A3's and 'A4's transferred to St Rollox shed – a quite unprecedented step. In addition, three 'A4's were re-allocated from Haymarket to Aberdeen (Ferryhill) shed. The new schedules were introduced as planned on 18th June 1962, and despite the unfamiliarity of some of the enginemen and shed staff, the 'new' locomotives settled in well. In October 1963 the Pacifics at Glasgow and Aberdeen were supplemented by a number of 'A4's surplus to requirements in England, though some were at first stored as reserve power. These engines included No.60019 *Bittern* which was initially stored at Kittybrewster shed. No.60019 later became the last 'A4' to be granted a heavy repair, at Darlington Works in March 1965, and survived to the end of the class in September 1966. It is seen near Cove Bay, south of Aberdeen, with the 5.15pm Aberdeen to Glasgow during late June 1966.   *Derek Penney*

Trains travelling southwards from Perth are faced with a 15-mile long climb, much of it on a gradient of 1 in 100, until the summit is reached a mile south of Gleneagles. In this picture LNER 'A4' Class Pacific No.60024 *Kingfisher*, makes a splendid sight as it breasts the summit with the up 'Grampian', the 1.30pm Aberdeen to Glasgow, on 2nd July 1966. Unfortunately, by this time the number of 'A4's in traffic was down to three, Nos.60019 *Bittern*, 60024 *Kingfisher* and 60034 *Lord Faringdon*, and during most of July they were out of service for repair, which caused great disappointment to many enthusiasts who had made the pilgrimage north to see them in action. All three engines eventually reappeared, but No.60034 was withdrawn in August, leaving Nos.60019/24 to soldier on to the end. *Kingfisher* worked the 1.30pm ex-Aberdeen on at least one occasion during the last week of August, while on 30th/31st August *Bittern* was turned out for the 7.10am Aberdeen to Glasgow and 5.30pm return. On 3rd September, a commemorative special from Glasgow to Aberdeen and return was organised by the ScR, using *Bittern* as motive power. The trains were on the three-hour timing, with the usual intermediate stops. Ferryhill shed, where two other 'A4's were positioned for photography, was specially opened to visitors and all this for a bargain fare of £2! The real finale took place the following week however, when *Kingfisher* worked the 5.15pm from Aberdeen on 13th September, returning home the following day for the last time at the head of the 8.25am from Glasgow.

Paul Riley

The North British Railway had a fairly extensive route mileage across the border in Northumberland, one of its lines being the Border Counties branch from Riccarton Junction to Hexham via Reedsmouth, opened in 1862. The Wansbeck Valley Railway, a purely local company, proposed a line from Reedsmouth to Morpeth which opened for passengers on 1st May 1865, by which time it had been absorbed by the NBR. The latter company worked the line from the start, and ran three trains a day along the thinly inhabited route. After the Second World War the service was down to only two return trains a day, and, not surprisingly, BR withdrew the passenger service on 15th September 1952, although ramblers' specials continued to run. In November 1963 freight workings between Reedsmouth and Woodburn ceased, the remaining Woodburn to Morpeth section lasting until 3rd October 1966. Here, 'J27' Class 0-6-0 No.65874 is depicted shunting at Woodburn on a sunny 21st July 1966, a few months prior to the line's complete closure.

Roger Cruse

Right, above: Most locomotives ran around in appalling external condition during the last days of steam, but here is an exception, a commendably clean 'Britannia' Pacific, No.70015 *Apollo*, which is seen heading an eastbound parcels train near Micklehurst, on the LNWR Manchester to Leeds route across the Pennines. Micklehurst was located on a loop line, used mainly by goods trains, which ran up the eastern side of the Tame Valley between Stalybridge and Diggle, a section which closed completely on 29th October 1966, more than two months after this picture was taken on 18th August. This line, which used the original, single bore, Standedge tunnels, has since been partially converted to a footpath. At the time of this photograph *Apollo* was shedded at Stockport and generally maintained in presentable external condition. No.70015 was based at a wide variety of sheds during its career, including Old Oak Common in the 1950s and Trafford Park (Manchester) in the early 1960s, for working expresses over the Peak Route to London St. Pancras. It also spent a period at Llandudno Junction. Later in its life, *Apollo* was based at Crewe North and Carlisle Kingmoor prior to being moved to Stockport. It was sent back to Kingmoor depot and withdrawn from there in August 1967 after a little over sixteen years service.   *Brian Magilton*

Right, below: Class 'J37' 0-6-0 No.64620 undertakes a little shunting at Inverkeithing on 26th August 1966. This type was introduced by the North British Railway, which classified the engines 'S' Class, in 1914, and 104 engines were eventually built up to 1921. They were a tower of strength on freight workings, for which they were primarily designed, but had an excellent turn of speed on passenger duty when the need arose. This veteran lasted until the last days of Scottish steam in April 1967, being employed by Dundee shed on miscellaneous local trip workings and yard pilot work. The class travelled as far as Montrose, on the East Coast main line, and had regular turns along the Brechin and Inverbervie branches.   *Phil Lynch*

The Isle of Wight's railway system, with its vintage rolling stock and invariably immaculate motive power, was always a great favourite amongst enthusiasts. Despite the modest traffic potential, the island was well served by a network which, in days gone by, stretched from Bembridge, in the east, to Freshwater, on the west coast. A series of closures in the 1950s reduced the system considerably, and only the Ryde to Cowes/Ventnor routes survived into the 1960s. By this time, all services were powered by ageing LSWR 'O2' Class 0-4-4Ts, most of which had been shipped over to the island in Southern Railway days. Ryde was the focal point of operations and the railway ran along the pier to Pier Head station, which dated from July 1880, from where ferries departed to the mainland. There was also a pier tramway, which is visible on the left of the picture. No.20 *Shanklin* is depicted between Pier Head and Esplanade stations in September 1966. The island locomotives were fitted with Westinghouse air brakes and enlarged coal bunkers. No.20's donkey pump can be seen attached to the right of the smokebox. Steam bowed out with a flourish on 31st December 1966, when one of the last trains, a Locomotive Club of Great Britain railtour, was double-headed by a pair of the remaining 'O2's. One or two 'O2' Class engines continued at work on engineers' trains for a further three months.

Derek Huntriss

The 'Bournemouth Belle' was introduced in July 1931 and initially conveyed a Weymouth portion, which was detached at Bournemouth. The timings were 10.30am from Waterloo and departure from Bournemouth West was at 4.50pm. For the first few years, operation was largely confined to the summer period, but in 1936, when the worst of the world economic recession was over, it became a daily service to Bournemouth West, the Weymouth portion having been withdrawn. At this time the train was hauled by either a 'Lord Nelson' or 'King Arthur' Class 4-6-0. After the war, the most noticeable difference in the make-up of the train was the motive power, the first post-war service being powered by 'Merchant Navy' Class No.2ICl8 *British India Line* on 7th October 1946. During this period of austerity, a trip on the opulent 'Belle' enabled travellers to forget, at least for a couple of hours, bread rationing and other post-war deprivations. In the early 1950s there was a brief flirtation with diesel power, but this was short-lived and the 'Belle' remained steam-worked until Brush Type 4 diesels (later Class 47) were diagrammed from January 1967. Steam continued to appear however, and during the final week of steam traction the 'Belle' was steam worked on two occasions. Here, an indescribably filthy 'Merchant Navy' Class, No.35012 *United States Lines*, not to mention a blue/grey parcels van, mar the appearance of the otherwise immaculate up train near Sway on 10th September 1966.

Michael Mensing

'B1' Class 4-6-0 No.61021, by this time stripped of its *Reitbok* nameplates, rests between duties in the roundhouse at York shed in November 1966. The 'B1's were extremely versatile engines and their wide route availability ensured they could perform an almost unlimited range of duties throughout the LNER system. At the end of 1966, the allocation at York was down to fourteen locomotives, of which eight were 'B1' Class engines. Built in 1947, No.61021 survived in traffic for a further seven months, being withdrawn in June 1967 when York shed closed to steam traction. By the standards of most steam sheds at that time, York shed offered modern, light and airy accommodation, in contrast to many depots, some of which were in even worse condition than the locomotives they maintained. The premises were used by diesels for a time, but were later refurbished to house the National Railway Museum's exhibits.

Jim Winkley

Some of the most demanding duties towards the end of steam were the heavy iron ore trains from Tyne Dock, near South Shields, to the steelworks at Consett, County Durham, which was located 850 feet above sea level. These trains largely followed the route of the Stanhope & Tyne Railway, opened as long ago as 1834, but from Pelton to Annfield Plain they used a deviation, which was opened by the North Eastern Railway in 1896. Part of the route was served by a passenger service from Newcastle to Blackhill via Consett, but this was discontinued on 23rd May 1955. The iron ore trains were introduced in 1953, when production at Consett steel works was expanded, and consisted of merry-go-round block trains of up to eight 56-ton hopper wagons. Originally, these workings were handled by 'O1' Class 2-8-0s, banked by 'Q7' Class 0-8-0s where necessary, and without a doubt, the sight and sound of one of these trains charging up the route's 1 in 50 gradients must have been an experience to remember. A batch of BR Standard Class '9F's, specially modified for air brake operation of the wagons' discharge doors, was later allocated to Tyne Dock shed for these trains and these remained staple power until steam finished on 19th November 1966. To commemorate the end of steam No.92063 was turned out in immaculate condition and carried 'The Tyne Docker' headboard. It is seen here near South Pelaw. Sadly, despite the engine's sparkling appearance, it was withdrawn a few days later. The iron ore trains were turned over to diesel traction and diverted to run over the East Coast line, sections of the old route from Hedworth Lane, near Boldon, to Washington being subsequently abandoned.

Paul Riley

The end of an era at Shrewsbury on 4th March 1967 as BR Standard Class '4MT' 4-6-0 No.75021 poses for the cameras prior to working the 9.10am Paddington to Aberystwyth, the last down 'Cambrian Coast Express', onward to the Welsh coast. Two days later electric services from London to the West Midlands were inaugurated and through trains from Paddington to Birkenhead and the Welsh coast were withdrawn. The history of the 'Cambrian Coast Express' can be traced back to 1927, when it was introduced by the GWR. At that time the train departed from London at 10.10am and ran on Fridays and Saturdays only. It was a pity that BR could not provide a clean engine for this historic occasion. Apart from the smokebox door, which had presumably been smartened up by enthusiasts at the last minute, the locomotive was in a filthy condition.   *Bill Chapman*

When Southern Region steam ended on 9th July 1967 more than a third of the remaining locomotives were Bulleid Pacifics, which powered the lion's share of the steam-hauled passenger services from Waterloo to Bournemouth, Weymouth and Salisbury. Many of these engines were rebuilt examples, but a handful of unrebuilt engines also survived into 1967. One of these was No.34019 *Bideford* which is depicted passing Esher, with an up Bournemouth express in tow, shortly before its withdrawal from service in March of that year. The Bulleid Pacifics, particularly the unrebuilt engines, were very complex machines and it was to the credit of the shed staff that they were kept going for so long on the minimal maintenance standards which prevailed during the last years of steam. The 2-BIL/2-HAL electric units, forming part of a slow train from Portsmouth on the adjacent track, were pre-war types and therefore older than *Bideford*, which emerged from Brighton Works in December 1945.

Geoff Rixon

The 5¼ mile-long branch line from Brockenhurst was opened to Lymington Town in July 1858 and was extended to Lymington Pier in May 1884; ferries connected Lymington with Yarmouth, on the Isle of Wight. In 1938 the Southern Railway introduced one of the first 'Drive on, Drive off' ferry services on this route. For many years the branch was push-pull worked by LSWR 'M7' Class 0-4-4Ts, but towards the end of their lives many of the 'M7's were worn out and – doubtless to the relief of the enginemen – their reign on the Lymington branch ended in June 1964. From that time more variety of motive power was seen on the line, with Ivatt 2-6-2Ts and BR Standard 2-6-4Ts to the fore, although BR Standard Class '3MT' 2-6-2Ts and Class '4MT' 2-6-0s could also be observed. In the summer months there was a through train from Waterloo, which was latterly hauled by 'Schools' Class 4-4-0s as far as Brockenhurst, where 'Q' Class 0-6-0s took over. The 4-4-0s, however, were used for the last time in 1962. The line eventually became the last steam worked passenger branch in Great Britain. This picture shows Ivatt 2-6-2T No.41320 leaving Lymington Pier with the 3.50pm departure on 26th March 1967, shortly before diesel units, which were a stopgap measure until electrification, took over on 3rd April.

Roger Cruse

'An elevated, mountainous and occasionally precipitous district'. These were the words of Josias Jessop, an engineer who was engaged to construct the Cromford and High Peak Railway across the Derbyshire moors in the 1820s. It was intended that the line would connect the Cromford canal with the Peak Forest canal at Whaley Bridge and the line was opened in 1831. The result was a unique and fascinating line, which tended to go up hills rather than around them, and the route originally incorporated nine spectacular inclines. Minerals from the local quarries were the staple traffic, particularly limestone. For many years the line was worked by former North London Railway 0-6-0Ts, but these were withdrawn in the late 1950s, when 'J94' Class 0-6-0STs took over The last rope-worked inclines in use were at Middleton and Sheep Pasture. In this picture a pair of 'J94's, Nos.68006 and 68012, are seen storming Hopton Incline – which had some sections as steep as 1 in 14 – on 30th April 1967, the very last day of this remarkable line.

Neville Simms

The last appearance of a steam locomotive at the head of a Royal train occurred on 30th May 1967, when HRH the Duke of Edinburgh travelled overnight from Windsor to Nidd Bridge, north of Harrogate. In order to provide heat, 'Jubilee' No.45562 *Alberta* hauled the train from York to Nidd Bridge, where the Duke slept overnight. After he had alighted, the train proceeded as empty stock to Ripon, where No.45562 ran round. When this manoeuvre was completed, *Alberta* hauled the stock tender-first back to York. In this shot, an immaculate No.45562 is depicted hauling the empty carriages northwards from Nidd Bridge to Ripon in the morning sunshine. By this time the line northwards from Ripon had been reduced to one operational single track, which explains why the train appears to be travelling on the wrong line. *Alberta* survived to become the last 'Jubilee' in traffic and it is to be regretted that this 'Royal' engine was later broken-up for scrap.

Peter Fitton

A very rare colour view of a Bulleid Pacific working a Weymouth to Westbury train of 'perishables' (probably tomatoes from the Channel Islands) past Maiden Newton, on 31st May 1967. Motive power was provided by 'West Country' Class No.34040 *Crewkerne* which was in quite presentable external condition. Maiden Newton was the junction for Bridport and the track of this branch, which was closed in May 1975, can be seen in the foreground. On the very last day of SR steam, 9th July 1967, very few workings occurred and it was, perhaps, ironic that much of the steam activity on that day was concentrated on the largely WR route from Weymouth to Westbury. The WR had been devoid of steam for more than a year by this date, but even so three special 'perishables' trains operated to Westbury, employing two Bulleid Pacifics and a BR Standard Class '5MT'.

Roger Cruse

Just over a month before the end of steam in Scotland, the Scottish Region organised a marathon railtour, which ran on 25th March 1967. Formed of a mammoth eighteen coach load, the train started in Edinburgh and ran to Carlisle via the Waverley route, using diesel traction. It then proceeded northwards to Perth with the same motive power, where Class '5MT' 4-6-0 No.44997 piloting 'A4' No.60009 *Union of South Africa*, took over for the run to Aberdeen via Forfar. The train then continued to Keith and eventually reached Aviemore using diesel traction. After a run over the Highland main line to Perth, the Class '5MT' and 'A4' took over again, returning the excursionists to Edinburgh. Steam working officially ceased in Scotland from 1st May 1967, but despite being withdrawn from service, No.44997 was appropriated for steam heating purposes at Craigentinny carriage sidings, Edinburgh. During its stint the Class '5MT' apparently travelled between Craigentinny and St. Margarets shed under its own power, thus becoming one of the last, possibly *the* last, working engines based on the ScR. Here, No.44997 is seen in steam at St. Margarets shed on 10th June 1967 and the locomotive is still in quite clean condition after its railtour appearance.

K. M. Falconer

1967 was an extremely depressing year for steam fans, who witnessed the rapid elimination of steam traction from many parts of the country. One of the undoubted highlights of the year though, was the employment of the last LMSR 'Jubilee' Class 4-6-0s, based at Leeds Holbeck shed, on summer Saturday extra trains over the Settle and Carlisle line. Two expresses were rostered for steam haulage, the 10.17am Leeds to Glasgow (6.40am ex-Birmingham) and the 9.20am St Pancras to Glasgow. The latter was not booked to stop at Leeds, but changed engines outside the main station. Amidst bleak moorland scenery so typical of the S&C, this train is seen heading north behind No.45593 *Kolhapur* at Lunds, between Garsdale and Ais Gill summit, on 19th August 1967. A parapet of Lunds viaduct is just visible, while the northern portal of Moorcock tunnel, in the background, is partly hidden by the locomotive's exhaust.

Derek Penney

Dent station, on the legendary Settle to Carlisle line, is the unmistakable location of this picture of an empty anhydrite train from Widnes to Long Meg sidings, north of Appleby. Motive power was provided by an unidentified BR Standard Class '9F' 2-10-0 and the picture was taken in late August 1967. The S&C had been largely neglected by steam enthusiasts who were probably deterred by its remoteness, sparsity of traffic, especially compared to the West Coast line, and inhospitable climate. In the summer of 1967 however, the route was invaded by hundreds of photographers who were attracted by the exploits of the last-surviving 'Jubilees'. Undoubtedly, the Class '8F's and '9F's, which worked the 'Long Megs' were the most spectacular performers on freight duty, powering very heavy trains up the fifteen miles-long climb from Ormside to Ais Gill summit, 1,169 feet above sea level. This was a challenging assignment for any locomotive, but by this time many engines were in a neglected condition and could often be seen struggling up to the summit at walking pace, wreathed in leaking steam. Steam haulage of these trains finished at the end of December 1967, when Carlisle Kingmoor depot was closed.   *Derek Penney*

The north-east of England was the birthplace of railways, but on 9th September 1967 main line steam in the area ended 150 years after the first successful locomotives ran. Nearly all regular passenger trains had been diesel-worked for some years, but steam survived on coal traffic at Blyth, Sunderland and West Hartlepool. The north-east was home, too, to the last pre-grouping engines on BR, the 'J27' 0-6-0s and 'Q6' 0-8-0s. The latter class were first introduced by the North Eastern Railway as class 'T2' and between 1913

and 1921 a total of 120 were built. In this memorable picture, 'Q6' Class No.63395 is seen pounding up Seaton Bank, parts of which are graded at 1 in 42, in fine style with the 11.15am coal empties from Sunderland South Dock to South Hetton Colliery on 7th September 1967, during the final week of steam operation. It was one of three 'Q6's which lasted until the end and No.63395 was later purchased for preservation on the North Yorkshire Moors Railway.

David Clark

One of the most interesting lines at the end of steam working in the north-east was the heavily-graded Silksworth colliery branch, just south of Sunderland. It was worked by 'J27's which were introduced by the North Eastern Railway as class 'P3' from 1906. A total of 105 locomotives was constructed before the grouping, a further ten being built in 1923. All these engines remained in service at nationalisation. Viewed from the top of a pit spoil heap, No.65894, the last 'J27' to be built, in 1923, is seen making a spectacular assault on the climb to the colliery with a train of empty wagons on 8th September 1967. This was the final day of steam working on this hitherto obscure branch and the locomotive's crew – evidently 'playing to the gallery' – provided a dramatic smoke effect for the benefit of lineside photographers. This fine old engine was later preserved by the North Eastern Locomotive Preservation Group.

David Clark

The weekend of 30th September/1st October 1967 was the last for ER steam in the West Riding of Yorkshire. Holbeck, Normanton and Low Moor sheds lost their steam allocations from 2nd October, leaving Royston, the last steam shed on the ER, to soldier on for a few more weeks. Normanton retained servicing facilities to cater for steam locomotives working across the Pennines from the LMR. With the closures, came the withdrawal of large numbers of engines and the extinction of the 'Jubilees', Austerity 2-8-0s plus the Stanier and Fairburn 2-6-4Ts. The weekend saw the last ordinary 'Jubilee' working over the Settle and Carlisle line, and the final steam-hauled passenger trains from Bradford Exchange to Leeds and a 'Jubilee' hauled parcels train from Leeds to Heysham. As if all this was not enough, there was even a railtour over the S&C involving preserved engines *Clun Castle* and *Sir Nigel Gresley*. The dubious honour of powering the very last BR steam train from Bradford fell to Fairburn Class '4MT' No.42152, which hauled the 4.18pm to Kings Cross, as far as Leeds, on 1st October. The 'Yorkshire Pullman' was also steam worked for the last time, appropriately by the last active 'B1' Class 4-6-0 No.61306 of Low Moor shed, which is seen in this photograph climbing out of Bradford, near Laisterdyke, on 30th September.

Jim Winkley

One of the most dramatic sights during the last years of steam was that of a train ascending the bank from Tebay to Shap Summit, in Westmorland, which is 916 feet above sea level. During 1967, steam was still prominent on many freight and van trains along the northern section of the West Coast main line, and in the summer of that year many holiday relief trains were also steam powered. But rapid dieselisation was taking place and at the end of the year Kingmoor depot at Carlisle, which had been the northern limit of steam operation, was closed and the stirring sight and sound of a train struggling up to Shap Summit had gone for ever. You can almost feel the cold in this superb study of BR Standard 'Britannia' Pacific No.70024 *Vulcan* and Class '4MT' No.75030 heaving a northbound freight up the 1 in 75 past Greenholme on an icy 20th December 1967, just over a week before steam finished.

Peter Fitton

With snow clinging to the gullies on the hillside, Stanier Class '8F' 2-8-0 No.48247 approaches Copy Pit summit, between Todmorden and Burnley, with a westbound coal train on 24th February 1968. Note the banker at the rear of the train. This line suffered the loss of its stopping passenger services in the late 1950s, but remained open for freight and seasonal holiday trains between Yorkshire and the Lancashire coast. The route traversed some rugged Pennine scenery and was very steeply graded, with westbound trains being faced with almost four miles of 1 in 65 from Stansfield Hall, near Todmorden, to the summit – a stern test for any locomotive. Class '8F' No.48278 brought down the curtain on steam over Copy Pit when it returned to Rose Grove shed 'light engine' at lunchtime on 3rd August 1968. Freight traffic has since declined dramatically on this route, primarily as a result of the run-down of the coal industry, but passenger services have seen a revival and regular Leeds to Blackpool services now run this way, so the line's future seems assured.

Paul Riley

Following the cessation of steam working to Carlisle at the end of December 1967, the attention of enthusiasts turned to the area south-east of Manchester, where steam was still employed on freight duties along part of the Midland Railway's highly scenic Manchester to Derby main line through the Derbyshire Peak District. Steam still handled goods traffic from the Manchester area to Buxton and a large limeworks complex at Peak Forest, just south of the 1,224 yards-long Dove Holes tunnel. The area abounded in fierce gradients, with southbound trains facing an almost continuous climb, much of it at 1 in 90, all the way from the Manchester suburbs to a summit at Peak Forest, from where the line descended to Derby on similar gradients. In this view, Class '8F' No.48775 is seen in an attractive setting, threading Ashwood Dale, between Peak Forest and Buxton, with a freight for Buxton on 28th February 1968, a few days prior to the closure of Buxton shed and the end of steam traction in the area. No.48775 was a widely travelled machine, seeing war service in Persia before returning to England at the end of hostilities. It eventually entered BR stock in 1957, only to be withdrawn by the Scottish Region in late 1962. It was reinstated by the LMR in September 1963 and survived until the end of steam.

Peter Fitton

The history of the boat expresses from Manchester can be traced back to 1874, when the North Lancashire Steam Navigation Company, which operated a twice-weekly Fleetwood to Belfast service, was taken over jointly by the L&YR and LNWR. From about that time a regular boat train service, initially hauled by Ramsbottom 2-4-0s, ran from Manchester to connect with sailings from Fleetwood. On 30th April 1928 the departure point was changed to Heysham. After the Second World War, Carnforth-based 'Jubilees' worked the service, until the rather unreliable Metrovick Co-Bo diesel locomotives took over in about 1963. But steam often substituted and, in 1965, BR realised their mistake and reintroduced steam traction with a Carnforth Class '5MT' being rostered – a rare case of a regular diesel-hauled service reverting to steam. This train was the last named express on BR to be regularly steam-worked and was usually formed of a rake of coaching stock in uniform livery – latterly a blue and grey set. Here, the final steam-hauled 'Belfast Boat Express' is seen near Adlington, with No.45025 (now preserved) in charge, on the morning of Sunday 5th May 1968. On Sunday evenings there was no sailing from Heysham, so the train from Manchester, which was not named, terminated at Morecambe.

Peter Fitton

LMSR Class '5MT' No.45310 awaits departure from Leeds with the 3.32am train to Halifax. Similar scenes must have been repeated on hundreds of occasions over the years, but this working, photographed on 18th May 1968, was the very last booked BR steam turn across the Pennines and, therefore, earned a place in the history books. On arrival at Halifax, the locomotive would be scheduled to take over the 2.10am from York, which departed from Halifax at 4.38am, to Manchester Victoria. This train usually conveyed a motley collection of vans, plus a solitary Brake Second Corridor coach for the few passengers on offer at such an uncivilised early hour. Towards the end of steam, the train became a favourite amongst the railway enthusiast fraternity and, on at least one occasion, conveyed unofficial buffet 'facilities' in the form of a crate of Newcastle Brown Ale, which was no doubt just the job at four o'clock in the morning!

Bill Chapman

The handful of passenger trains in the north-west of England which remained steam-hauled at the start of the summer timetable on 6th May 1968, included the Manchester portion of the Glasgow to Liverpool/Manchester sleeping car train which was booked for an LMSR Class '5MT' 4-6-0 from Wigan (North Western) to Manchester (Exchange). These workings continued after BR had prematurely announced the end of steam on passenger duties from 6th May, so the locomotive diagrams were hurriedly revised from 20th May with the result that just two Saturday only workings remained after that date. In this picture the empty stock of the last steam-hauled sleeping car train is seen passing through Manchester (Victoria) presumably *en route* from Exchange station to Red Bank carriage sidings on 18th May 1968. Motive power was provided by Class '5MT' No.45055 which was immediately recognised by the rather crudely painted number on its smokebox door.   *Bill Chapman*

The 10¾ mile-long Skipton to Grassington branch opened in 1902 as the Yorkshire Dales Railway, but was worked by the Midland Railway from the outset. At one time there were grandiose plans to build a line to connect Skipton with the North Eastern Railway south of Darlington, but, not surprisingly, nothing came of this scheme. The Grassington line, which had only one intermediate station, at Rylstone, served a sparsely inhabited area and lost its regular passenger service as early as 22nd September 1930, although ramblers' excursions continued well into BR days. In the late 1960s this hitherto relatively unknown line gained a higher profile, due to the continued use of steam traction on stone trains from Swinden quarry. In this picture BR Standard Class '4MT' 4-6-0 No.75019, which was kept in spotless external condition by local enthusiasts, is seen making an energetic departure from the quarry on 25th May 1968.

Jim Winkley

Sunset of British steam? On the last weekday of BR steam operation, Friday 2nd August 1968, Class '5MT' No.44781 was photographed at Arnside, crossing the River Kent estuary in splendid silhouette, with the 8.28pm Barrow to Preston van train. The locomotive spent the following day at Lostock Hall shed being prepared for railtour duties on Sunday 4th August when it piloted *Oliver Cromwell* for a part of the day. A week later, paired with sister engine No.44871, it powered the last BR steam-hauled train over the Settle and Carlisle line. Alas, after its starring role on the BR special, No.44781 had a bizarre end. It was disguised as a tank engine for the film 'The Virgin Soldiers', derailed and 'wrecked', and later broken-up on site after the cameras had done their job. No.44781 was one of 241 'Black Fives' built at Crewe Works, from where it emerged in August 1947.

John Scrace